Great Minds of Science

# Antoine Lavoisier

## Founder of Modern Chemistry

*Revised Edition*

Lisa Yount

**Enslow Publishers, Inc.**
40 Industrial Road
Box 398
Berkeley Heights, NJ 07922
USA

http://www.enslow.com

*For my brother, Stuart*

**Library of Congress Cataloging-in-Publication Data**

Yount, Lisa.
  Antoine Lavoisier : founder of modern chemistry / Lisa Yount. — Rev. ed.
      p. cm. — (Great minds of science)
  Summary: "A biography of eighteenth-century French chemist Antoine
Lavoisier and includes related activities for readers"—Provided by publisher.
  Includes bibliographical references and index.
  ISBN-13: 978-0-7660-3011-4
  ISBN-10: 0-7660-3011-3
  1. Lavoisier, Antoine Laurent, 1743–1794—Juvenile literature. 2. Chemists—
France—Biography—Juvenile literature. I. Title.
  QD22.L4Y68 2008
  540.92—dc22
  [B]
                                    2007020299

Printed in the United States of America

10 9 8 7 6 5 4 3 2 1

**To Our Readers:** We have done our best to make sure all Internet Addresses
in this book were active and appropriate when we went to press. However,
the author and the publisher have no control over and assume no liability
for the material available on those Internet sites or on other Web sites they
may link to. Any comments or suggestions can be sent by e-mail to
comments@enslow.com or to the address on the back cover.

♻ Enslow Publishers, Inc., is committed to printing our books on recycled
paper. The paper in every book contains 10% to 30% post-consumer waste
(PCW). The cover board on the outside of each book contains 100% PCW. Our
goal is to do our part to help young people and the environment too!

**Illustration Credits:** Stephen Delisle, pp. 11, 112; Courtesy E.E. Smith
Collection, Special Collection, Van Pelt-Dietrich Library Center, University of
Pennsylvania, pp. 15, 28, 33, 42, 46, 53, 76, 89, 102; The Granger Collection,
New York, pp. 8, 20, 31, 40, 63, 77, 79; Jupiterimages Corporation/Photos.com,
pp. 59, 72; Mary Evans Picture Library/Everett Collection, p. 85; SPL/Photo
Researchers, Inc., p. 25.

**Cover Illustration:** The Granger Collection, New York (foreground);
Jupiterimages Corporation/Photos.com (background).

# Contents

# Introduction: Recipes for Revolution

WHEN YOU EAT A CAKE, YOU DO NOT have to know what is in it in order to enjoy it. If you want to *make* a cake, though, you need a recipe. The recipe tells you what things go into the cake, such as eggs and flour, and how much of each thing you need. It also tells you what to do when you make the cake—which things to mix together and when to add them. Finally, it tells you how long to bake the cake and at what temperature.

Chemistry had few good recipes two hundred fifty years ago. Chemistry is the study of different kinds of matter, or substances. It shows what they are made of and how they change when they are combined. (Substances in a cake combine and change when they cook. That is why a baked cake looks different from an unbaked one.) Scientists who study chemistry are called chemists.

Eighteenth-century chemists knew how to make some kinds of compounds, or combined substances. They knew some of the changes that took place when substances were combined. However, they did not know why most of these changes happened nor how to make sure that certain changes would occur.

Even the names that chemists used for substances were confusing. Most of the names came from ancient times, when chemistry was seen as a kind of magic. The names told little about what compounds the substances contained.

A French chemist named Antoine Lavoisier (an-TWAHN luv-WAHZ-ee-ay) changed all that in the late 1700s. He created names for compounds that told what was in them. He showed chemists how to write recipes that described exactly how substances combined. Most important, he put what chemists knew into a new system. In a sense, he made the first modern chemistry cookbook. His system greatly changed the way chemists thought and worked. He was right in calling it "a revolution in . . . chemistry."[1]

Lavoisier also made important discoveries. He showed what happened when substances burned. He showed that air and water were made of other substances. (Before then, chemists had thought air and water were elements. An element cannot be broken down into other materials.) He also found out about the chemistry of living things. He showed what happens when animals breathe, for instance.

Lavoisier tried to help the people of France. For example, he used science to find better ways of farming, improved the gunpowder that France used in wars, and tried to make taxes fairer. He lived at a time, however, when making useful changes in the country was hard.

During most of Lavoisier's life, France was ruled by a king. The king and his court wasted money and treated the French people badly.

Antoine Lavoisier caused a revolution in chemistry. Sadly, in 1794, a political revolution took his life. This drawing was made a short time before his execution.

The people rebelled against him in 1789. Three years later, they made France a republic.

Lavoisier advised the leaders of both the old and the new governments. Sad to say, neither listened to most of his ideas. Worse still, the new French leaders tried to destroy all who had worked for the old system. They killed many innocent people. Lavoisier was one of them.

His work lives on, though. Chemists still use his system of naming substances. They still use his way of writing chemical recipes, and they still believe most of his ideas about burning and breathing. For these reasons, Antoine Lavoisier has been called the father of modern chemistry.

# Set for Success

ANTOINE LAVOISIER'S FAMILY HAD worked their way up in the world. Long ago they were peasant farmers. Then, about 150 years before Antoine's birth, one Lavoisier became a coachman for the French king. Later Lavoisiers were a postman, a policeman, and a merchant. Antoine's grandfathers were both lawyers, and so was his father, Jean Antoine. They were rich and respected men.

The Lavoisiers had also worked their way to Paris. The family came from a country town called Villers-Cotterets, but Antoine's father had moved to Paris, the French capital. Paris was smelly and noisy. Travel through its dark, narrow streets could be dangerous. Still, it also had

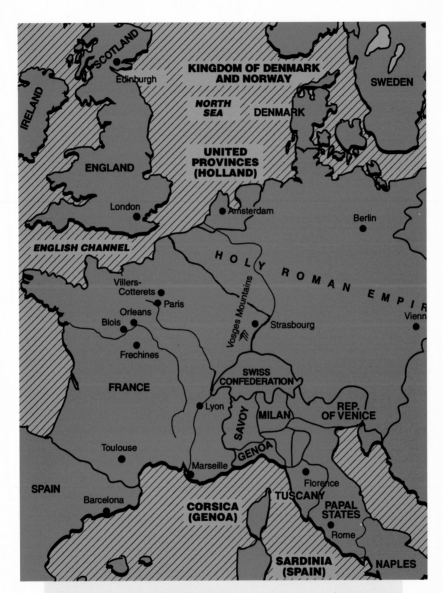

France was one of the most powerful nations in eighteenth-century Europe (above). Lavoisier increased France's power by improving its supply of gunpowder.

broad avenues and fine buildings. Most Parisians thought it was the best place in the world to live.

## A Privileged Youth

Antoine Laurent Lavoisier was born on August 26, 1743. As a rich family's only son, he seemed sure of an easy life. Money could not stop tragedy, though. Antoine's mother, Emilie, died when he was just five years old. His younger sister, Marie, died when he was a teenager.

After Emilie Lavoisier passed away, Antoine and his father and sister moved in with Emilie's mother, Madame (Mrs.) Frere Punctis. Emilie's sister, Constance, also lived there. Grandmother Punctis and Aunt Constance helped raise the two children. Antoine and his father also grew close. Antoine later called him "my best friend."[1]

When Antoine was eleven, he started school at the Collège des Quatre-Nations (College of Four Nations). It was sometimes called Collège Mazarin, after the man who founded it. Antoine's first classes there were like those of a high school. He learned writing, public speaking, Greek, Latin, and French literature. His work won several prizes. In his last year, he also took science and math courses. Most schools did not have such courses, but those at Collège Mazarin were said to be the best in France.

## Learning About Science

As a young man, Antoine Lavoisier studied law because his lawyer father expected him to do so. In his spare time, though, Lavoisier learned more about science. For instance, he learned geology, or earth science, from Jean Guettard, a famous scientist who was also a family friend.

Lavoisier learned chemistry from Guillaume Rouelle, who gave public lectures on the subject. Rouelle grew excited when he did experiments for the crowd. He tossed away his hat, then his wig. His coat and vest soon followed. His love for his work was catching.

Lavoisier liked Rouelle. He was less pleased with chemistry, though. He wrote later that chemistry in those days "was founded on only a few facts. . . . [It] was composed of . . .

incoherent [confused] ideas and unproven suppositions. . . . I realized I would have to begin the study of chemistry all over again."[2]

In the century before, men such as Isaac Newton had changed the way scientists worked. They learned to do more than dream up ideas. They tested their beliefs with experiments. They tried to make sure nature really acted the way they thought it would. Lavoisier wanted chemists to do more of this. "We must trust to nothing but facts," he wrote later. "These are presented to us by Nature, and cannot deceive."[3]

Lavoisier won his law degree in 1764. He never worked as a lawyer, though. Instead, he set out to make his name in science.

The best French scientists belonged to the Royal Academy of Sciences. Only fifty-four men could be in this group. A new member could join only when an old one died. The academy chose its members, but the king had to approve them. Most scientists were elected only after long careers. Lavoisier did not plan to wait. He made sure the academy noticed him right away.

**When Lavoisier first learned chemistry, a chemist's laboratory looked like this.**

Scientists shared their research by reading papers at academy meetings. The papers were later published. It was an honor for nonmembers to present papers. Lavoisier presented his first one in 1765, when he was just twenty-two years old. By the standards of the time, he was not yet an adult. Lavoisier's paper was about a mineral called gypsum, which was used to make a kind of plaster.

The next year, Lavoisier won the academy's attention in another way. The streets of Paris needed better lighting at night. The academy offered a prize to the person who suggested the best way to light the streets. Lavoisier decided to enter the contest.

He carefully studied each kind of lighting. He looked at different sizes and types of lamps, tested oils and candles that might burn in them, and measured the distance each kind of light could cover. He worked out what each would cost. He put all of his results into his contest entry.

The academy sorted the contest entries into two groups. One group made practical suggestions. The other looked at the lighting problem as a whole. The academy split the prize money among the three best papers in the practical group. The scientists decided that Lavoisier's paper was the best in the other group. They gave him a gold medal for it.

Lavoisier went on his only long field trip in 1767, a year after he had won his medal. Jean Guettard decided to go to the Vosges Mountains to get data for a geological map of France that he was making. The mountains were on the other side of France, near the Swiss border. Guettard asked Lavoisier to come with him.

For more than four months the two men

traveled through the countryside. They tested soil, minerals, and water. They sampled products of farms and industries. During this trip, Lavoisier saw for the first time what an unhappy life most French peasants led.

## The Tax Farm

In 1768, Lavoisier joined two groups that would shape the rest of his life. First, he was elected to the Academy of Sciences on May 18. At twenty-four, he was one of the youngest members ever.

The second group was a business firm known as the *Ferme-Générale*. Its sixty leaders were called Farmers-General. To most people, it was the Tax Farm.

The government farmed out, or leased, to this company the right to collect certain taxes. These included sales taxes on products such as salt and tobacco. The Tax Farm collected taxes on goods from foreign countries. It could also tax goods moved from one part of France to another.

The Tax Farm paid the government a certain amount of money each year. The farm collected as much tax as it could. Sometimes it took in more than it had paid. The farmers could keep this extra money.

The Farmers-General hired agents to collect the taxes. The agents could search homes and have people arrested. Some abused these powers. Some Farmers-General also kept money they had no right to keep. Others tried to do their jobs as honestly as they could. Lavoisier planned to be honest.

The French people hated all the tax farmers, honest or not. No one likes a tax collector, especially when the taxes seem unfair, and these did. People had to pay the salt tax even when they bought no salt, for instance. Worst of all, rich nobles paid no tax at all.

Lavoisier saw the Tax Farm as a good way to invest money. He felt he could make a profit even if he was honest. He used money that his mother had left him to buy a third of a share in the farm. An older Farmer-General named

Baudon owned the rest. When Baudon died in 1779, Lavoisier took on the whole share. He then became a Farmer-General.

Joining the Tax Farm proved to be more than a good investment for Lavoisier. He became friends with a Farmer-General named Jacques Paulze, who had a young daughter named Marie Anne. A powerful relative wanted Marie to marry a middle-aged friend of his, but she called the man "a fool . . . and an ogre."[4]

In those days, parents often arranged their children's marriages. Still, Paulze did not want to make Marie marry a man she hated. The best way to escape the relative's pressure, he thought, was for Marie to marry someone else quickly. He asked Lavoisier to be the groom.

Red-haired Lavoisier was young and handsome. Marie was small and pretty, with brown hair and blue eyes. They liked each other and agreed to the wedding. They were married on December 16, 1771. Lavoisier was twenty-eight, and Marie was just fourteen. It was not

Lavoisier and his wife, Marie, had a very happy marriage. She helped him by taking notes during his experiments and drawing pictures for his books. A famous French artist, Jacques Louis David, painted this picture of them.

uncommon in those days for a bride to be so young. Life spans were much shorter then.

Lavoisier and his wife turned out to be perfectly matched. In later years, Marie learned chemistry and became her husband's assistant. She took notes when he did experiments and drew pictures for his books. She learned English so she could translate papers in that language for him. She entertained the many scientists who came to see him. One called her "a lively, sensible, scientific lady."[5]

By the time he was twenty-eight, Antoine Lavoisier seemed to have all he could want. He had a pretty, intelligent wife. He had money from his family and a chance to make more from the Tax Farm. He had done scientific research. Most important to him, he had been accepted by the Academy of Sciences. With such a fine start, his life seemed sure to be a great success.

# Fire and Air

IN ANCIENT TIMES, GREEK THINKERS claimed that there were just four elements: earth, air, fire, and water. Unlike other substances, the Greeks said, these elements could not be taken apart or broken down. A form of this theory was still popular when Lavoisier began studying chemistry, although it had been modified over the centuries. In time, Lavoisier would work with each of these "elements" except earth. He would show that they were not elements at all.

## Heating Brings Changes

Lavoisier started his studies with water. Chemists thought water could change into earth, and Lavoisier decided to test that idea. First, he weighed an empty glass vessel. Then he put clean water in it, sealed the vessel, and weighed it again. Next, he heated the water until it was just below boiling temperature. He kept it that way for 101 days. After a while, flakes of powder appeared in the water.

Lavoisier finally let the vessel cool and weighed it. The total weight had not changed. Then he opened the vessel. He weighed the vessel, the water, and the powder separately. The water's weight was the same as before, but Lavoisier found that the vessel had lost a bit of weight. The missing weight was about the same as the weight of the powder. Lavoisier decided that the powder must have come from the vessel's glass. Water could not be changed to earth after all! Lavoisier told the Academy of Sciences about his experiment on November 14, 1770.

Lavoisier would later learn more about water. Next, though, his mind turned to fire and air. With other scientists, he used a device called a burning-glass to heat diamonds to a very high temperature. The burning-glass was like a huge magnifying glass in a frame. A magnifying glass can start a fire by focusing sunlight. The burning-glass worked the same way.

When a diamond was heated in the air, it vanished. Lavoisier found that the gem was not changed, though, if heated in a vacuum. This suggested that the diamonds could burn. Chemists knew that substances could burn only in air.

Lavoisier decided to learn what happened to air during burning, or combustion. Until then, most chemists had not studied air carefully. They knew it was needed for some chemical reactions, including burning. (In a reaction, two or more substances combine and change each other.) They did not think air took part in the reactions, though.

In 1772, Lavoisier studied substances called phosphorus and sulfur. Both burn easily. When they burn, they form acids. An acid is a sour substance, like vinegar or lemon juice. Lavoisier found that the acids weighed more than the phosphorus and sulfur had before they were

Lavoisier used a burning-glass like this one to find out what happened when diamonds were heated. The burning glass focused sunlight to produce a very high temperature.

burned. He thought the added weight must have come from the air. When the substances burned, he guessed that air combined with them to form the acids.

Lavoisier also began to look at a second process that used fire and air. When metals are heated in air, a powder or ash forms on them. This process was named calcining, and the powder was called calx. Some metals do not need heat to calcine. When iron rusts, for instance, a red powder forms. It is a calx. Chemists guessed that calcining was a kind of slow combustion.

Chemists of Lavoisier's time thought fire could act like a chemical substance. In the early 1700s, a German chemist, Georg Stahl, named this substance phlogiston. No one had seen or measured phlogiston, but all things that burned were said to contain it. Substances that burned easily and left almost nothing behind, such as oil and charcoal, were thought to be almost pure phlogiston.

When substances burned or calcined, phlogiston was supposed to be forced out of them. There was just one problem with this idea: the calx made from a metal weighed more than the metal had. If something left the metal when the calx was made, how could the calx be heavier? Lavoisier suspected that the metal joined with air to form the calx. The air supplied the weight that the calx gained.

Calcining also worked in reverse. When a calx was heated with charcoal, the charcoal vanished and the metal reappeared. Chemists thought the charcoal gave its phlogiston to the calx. The two combined to make the metal. If Lavoisier was right, though, air should be released when the metal formed.

Lavoisier tested his guess with calces of the metals lead and tin. (*Calces* is the plural of *calx*.) He found that a large amount of gas bubbled out when the calces changed into metals. He thought the gas was air. He did not know there were other kinds of gas.

## Different Kinds of Air

Soon after, though, Lavoisier learned that some British chemists had found what they thought were different kinds of air. For instance, a Scottish chemist named Joseph Black had discovered what he called "fixed air" in 1754. This gas bubbled off when Black put chalk

Georg Stahl, a German scientist, said that fire could act like a chemical substance. He called this substance phlogiston.

in acid. Black thought the air was fixed, or firmly attached, to the chalk until the acid released it. Fixed air was also released when charcoal burned or animals breathed.

Several tests showed that fixed air was not the same as common air. A candle would not burn in fixed air, for instance. A mouse would die if put in a jar of it. Today we know that Black's fixed air is carbon dioxide.

Lavoisier decided to find out whether the air that took part in burning and calcining was a special kind. On February 20, 1773, he wrote that he thought these experiments would "bring about a revolution in physics and in chemistry."[1]

Lavoisier began by repeating the experiments that Black and others had done on air. He used "new safeguards" to make sure the results were correct. He wrote, "the results of the other authors [who had studied air] . . . appeared to me like separate pieces of a great chain; these authors have joined only some links of the chain. An immense series of experiments remains to be made in order to lead to a continuous whole."[2]

Lavoisier performed more experiments with calces next. He made a metal from a calx in a sealed vessel full of air and showed that about a fifth of the air disappeared in the process. This was true no matter how much metal he used. The weight of air lost was the same as the weight the calx gained. This proved that the calx took its added weight from the air. In 1774, Lavoisier described his experiments in his first book. In English, it was called *Physical and Chemical Tracts*. (Tracts are short papers.)

Lavoisier was starting to suspect that air was not an element, as chemists had always thought. Instead, it was a mixture of gases. Just one of these gases seemed to take part in calcining. But what gas was it?

## "The Purest Part of Air"

For a while, Lavoisier thought the gas was Black's fixed air. When a calx was heated with charcoal, a gas was released that met tests for fixed air. He began to change his mind, though, after an English scientist named Joseph Priestley came to dinner in October 1774.

Priestley had been a minister and teacher. He started studying chemistry in his spare time. His work with "airs" was known all over Europe. When he visited France, the Lavoisiers gave a dinner party for him. Priestley wrote later that "most of the philosophical [educated] people of the city [Paris] were present" at the party.[3]

During the dinner, Priestley told Lavoisier about some experiments he had done two months before. He had worked with a calx of mercury. (Mercury, a metal, is a silvery liquid at room temperature. It is used in some household thermometers.) Priestley found that the calx gave off an "air" as it turned back into metal. The gas could not be fixed air. Priestley said that "a candle burned much better [in it] than in

Joseph Priestley, a British scientist, discovered what was later called oxygen. He told Lavoisier about this gas at a party.

common air."[4] He called this gas "pure air." Later he said it was "dephlogisticated air," or air without phlogiston. He thought this air pulled phlogiston out of other substances. As a result, they burned well in it.

Priestley later wrote that the Lavoisiers "expressed great surprise" when he told them of his discovery.[5] Lavoisier was surprised because he, like others, thought the calx would give off fixed air. Then he remembered that mercury calx was special. Other calces turned back into metal only when charcoal was heated with them, but mercury calx did not need charcoal. The new gas thus had to have come from the calx.

Lavoisier repeated Priestley's experiments, then tested the gas that came from the mercury calx. He wrote later that "a taper [candle] burned in it with a dazzling splendour. . . . Charcoal, instead of consuming [burning] quietly, as it does in common air, burnt with a flame, attended with a decrepitating [sputtering] noise. . . . [It] threw out such a brilliant light that the eye could hardly endure it."[6]

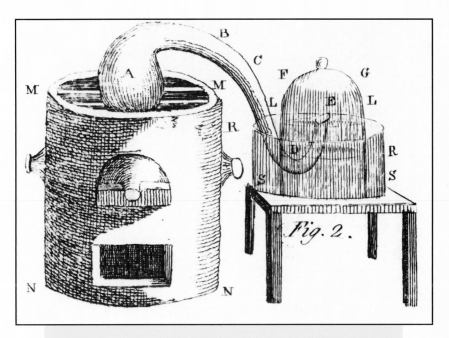

Lavoisier used this equipment to repeat Priestley's experiment. The large object on the left is a sort of oven. It heated mercury calx inside the curved vessel. Oxygen was given off when the calx turned back into mercury. The gas was collected in the bell-shaped jar on the right.

Lavoisier told the Academy of Sciences about his work on April 26, 1775. "The principle [substance] which combines with metals during their calcination," he claimed, was "the purest part of the air."[7] He went on to explain that mercury calx could be turned to metal with or without charcoal. When he used charcoal, he said, fixed air was produced during the reaction, and the charcoal vanished. "It follows," he said, "that . . . fixed air . . . results from the combination of the highly respirable part of the air with charcoal."[8]

Lavoisier called the new gas "highly respirable" because he had found that it was used in respiration, or breathing. Both he and Priestley had tried the gas on animals. They found that mice or birds lived longer in a jar of this gas than in one of common air. For a while, Lavoisier called the gas "vital [life-giving] air" because of this. Priestley even breathed the gas himself. "I fancied that my breast [chest] felt peculiarly light and easy for some time afterwards," he wrote.[9] He thought the gas might help people with lung disease.

Both men knew that respiration was really more than breathing. It was a chemical reaction that kept animals alive. No one understood it well. People knew that animals died if they could not breathe fresh air. Believers in the phlogiston theory thought this happened because animals breathed out phlogiston. They said that after a while, the air became so full of phlogiston that it could hold no more. Then the phlogiston was pushed back into the animals' lungs and killed them. Lavoisier, though, said animals died when their respiration used up Priestley's new "air." Only that part of common air was used in breathing. Respiration was like combustion and calcination in that way.

First Priestley, then Lavoisier came to realize that this new substance was more than just clean air. It was a separate gas. In 1777, Lavoisier proved that common air was a mixture of this gas and at least one other.

He did it by, so to speak, taking air apart and putting it back together. First, he heated mercury in a sealed vessel containing air for twelve days. The mercury slowly turned to calx, and about a sixth of the air disappeared. Flames went out in the gas that was left. Animals died when put in it. Clearly, the part of the air that supported life and burning had been removed.

In killing mice and putting out candles, the leftover gas acted like fixed air. Other tests, though, showed that it was not. We now know that this second gas was nitrogen.

Now Lavoisier removed the mercury calx he had made. He heated it in a new vessel, and it turned back into mercury. As it did, it released almost the same amount of gas that had vanished during the calcining. This gas acted like vital air. When Lavoisier combined it with the gas left from the first experiment, the mixture met tests for common air.

Lavoisier also showed that vital air combined with phosphorus and sulfur when they burned and formed acids. Indeed, he thought all acids were formed when nonmetals combined with vital air. Because of this, he named this gas oxygen, which means "acid former," in 1779. His belief that all acids contain oxygen proved to be wrong, but his conclusion that a substance combines with oxygen when it burns or calcines was correct. Today, scientists know that oxygen makes up about a fifth of common air. Most of the rest is nitrogen.

Lavoisier now had facts to support his theory that oxygen, not phlogiston, was important in burning, calcining, and respiration. He told the Academy of Sciences what he had found out in November 1777. At about the same time he wrote, "I am at the point of attacking the entire doctrine [set of ideas] . . . concerning phlogiston. . . . [I will] prove that it is erroneous [wrong] in every respect."[10] He seemed very sure of himself, but this task would prove difficult indeed.

# 3

# Down with Phlogiston

LAVOISIER GATHERED EVIDENCE TO
support his attack on phlogiston during the
early 1780s. He said that his ideas about
oxygen should replace the phlogiston theory.
Combustion, calcination, and respiration did not
happen because substances lost phlogiston, he
insisted. They happened because substances
combined with oxygen. He admitted he could
not disprove Stahl's idea completely, but he
believed that his own theory explained all
these reactions better. "Chemistry can be
explained in a satisfactory manner without the
need of phlogiston," he said. "That is enough to
render it infinitely likely that [phlogiston] does
not exist."[1]

Critics pointed out that Lavoisier's theory did

not explain some things. One was a gas that had been discovered in 1766 by another British scientist, Henry Cavendish. Cavendish called the gas "inflammable air" because it burned so fiercely. He thought it was pure phlogiston. It was later renamed hydrogen. Lavoisier could not show that this gas joined with oxygen when it burned. He could not tell what product its burning gave. He thought an acid should be formed, but he could not find any.

Several scientists had tried to find out what happened when inflammable air burned. They saw drops of clear liquid form inside the vessels where the burning took place, and they called this fluid "dew." In 1781, Cavendish showed that this dew was just what it looked like: water. He thought the water had been contained in the two gases.

As with oxygen, Lavoisier first heard of this discovery from a visitor. This time his guest was Charles Blagden, Cavendish's assistant. Blagden came to Paris in June 1783.

When Lavoisier heard Blagden's news, he

Henry Cavendish, another British scientist, discovered hydrogen. He also showed that water formed when hydrogen gas was burned. Only Lavoisier, though, realized that water was a combination of hydrogen and oxygen.

repeated Cavendish's experiments at once. He got the same results, but the results meant something different to Lavoisier. He thought that the two gases had combined to make the water. He pointed out that the water weighed as much as the combined weights of the gases. On November 12, 1783, he told the Academy of Sciences that water was not an element. It was made of hydrogen and oxygen.

Lavoisier had shown that air was not an element—that it contained several different substances—by taking it apart and putting it back together. He now did the same with water, but in reverse order. He had formed water from hydrogen and oxygen. Now he showed that water could be broken down into the same two gases. He heated iron and water and showed that hydrogen was set free. Meanwhile, the oxygen from the water combined with the iron to make iron calx, or rust.

This new understanding of water explained many reactions that the oxygen theory had not been able to account for. As a result, more and

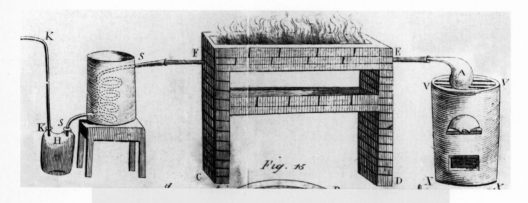

Lavoisier used this equipment to break water down into hydrogen and oxygen. The long straight tube is an iron gun barrel. It was made very hot in a charcoal fire (center). Water was passed through the tube. Oxygen from the water joined with the iron to make a rustlike powder. Hydrogen was released as a gas. It was collected in the vessel at the far right.

more scientists decided that Lavoisier's theory was correct.

## Studying Respiration

While he was learning about water, Lavoisier was also learning more about heat and respiration. He did this by using a new device called a calorimeter, which measures the heat given off by chemical reactions. It can also measure heat from an animal's body.

A friend of Antoine Lavoisier's, a famous mathematician named Simon Laplace, designed the calorimeter. Laplace based his design on something that Joseph Black had noticed. Normally, when heat is added to a substance, the substance's temperature rises. Black found, however, that this did not happen when heat turned ice into liquid water. The temperature of the water stayed the same until all the ice melted because all the heat energy was being used to melt the ice. The heat could thus be measured by measuring the amount of ice it melted.

Laplace's calorimeter had three metal containers, one inside the other. The innermost one held whatever was being tested. The middle container was filled with a weighed amount of ice. As the ice melted, water from it drained into a jar under the device. This water could later be weighed. The outer container held more ice or snow. It kept the room's heat from melting the ice in the middle container.

Between 1782 and 1784, Lavoisier and Laplace did many experiments with their calorimeter. Some measured the heat from burning and other reactions. In others, a guinea pig sat in the inner container. A tube carried in fresh air for the animal to breathe. Another tube removed the gas it breathed out. As the guinea pig sat there, its body heat melted ice in the middle container.

Once Lavoisier kept a guinea pig in the device for ten hours. He measured the amount of fixed air (carbon dioxide gas) that the animal breathed out in that time. He also weighed the water its body heat made from the ice. He found out how much charcoal he had to burn to make the same amount of fixed air. He compared the weight of the water made by the burning charcoal with the weight made by the guinea pig. The two were almost the same.

Lavoisier had already guessed that respiration was much like the burning of charcoal. Both used up oxygen. Both gave off carbon dioxide. The fact that they made about the same amount of heat, he thought, proved that they were the same. In June 1783, he wrote: "Respiration is . . . a combustion—a very slow one . . . but otherwise perfectly similar to that of . . . [charcoal]. It takes place in . . . the lungs. . . . The heat evolved [produced] . . . spreads into the blood which traverses [passes through] the lungs. . . . and from there it is distributed through the whole animal system."[2]

Once he learned how water was made, Lavoisier came to understand respiration even better. His calorimeter experiments showed that a guinea pig's body made a little more heat than burning charcoal. In 1785 he learned why. He found that an animal's breath contained water vapor (water as a gas) as well as carbon dioxide. He worked out how much heat was needed to make that much water from hydrogen and oxygen. That heat, added to the heat needed to make the carbon dioxide, equaled the body heat he had measured. In other words, respiration was really two combustions. One burned carbon, and the other burned hydrogen. Both substances came from the animal's body.

Lavoisier knew that birds and mammals

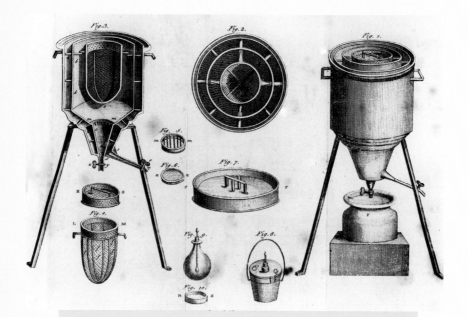

A friend of Lavoisier's, mathematician Simon Laplace, designed this device, called a calorimeter. It measured heat by measuring the amount of water formed by ice that the heat melted. Lavoisier used it to study animals' body heat and respiration.

could maintain their body temperatures no matter how cold the outside air became. He thought the heat made by respiration kept the animals warm. Basically, he was right.

Lavoisier's calorimeter studies were some of the first to measure chemical reactions in the bodies of living things. In doing them, Lavoisier made great strides in biology as well as in chemistry.

## Competing Theories

Lavoisier made his main attack on phlogiston in a paper he read to the Academy of Sciences in the summer of 1785. He called Stahl's theory "an error . . . fatal to chemistry."[3] Chemists used phlogiston in ways that contradicted each other, he pointed out. They could not agree on what phlogiston was. "Sometimes it has weight, sometimes it has not; sometimes it is free fire, sometimes it is fire combined with an earth; sometimes it passes through the pores of vessels, sometimes they are impenetrable to it. . . . It . . . changes its form every instant!"[4]

No real substance could act like this. Therefore, Lavoisier announced, "Stahl's phlogiston is imaginary."[5]

By that time, Lavoisier had been elected the director of the academy. Even so, "I do not expect that my ideas [about phlogiston] will be adopted at once," he admitted—and he was right.[6] A visiting Dutch chemist went to the Academy of Sciences meeting at which Lavoisier read his paper. At most such meetings the scientists listened politely to each other. The Dutchman wrote that this time, though, "violent objections" interrupted the reading.[7]

In Germany, Stahl's homeland, feelings were even stronger. When some German students heard about Lavoisier's paper, they burned straw figures of him. In France, however, Lavoisier had supporters as well as critics. These supporters were chemists, physicists, and mathematicians who visited Lavoisier often and became his friends. (Lavoisier was one of the few chemists of his time who tried to bring these three sciences closer together.) They explained his ideas in letters to other scientists and repeated his experiments for visitors. Their work during the rest of the 1780s helped Lavoisier slowly win the war of ideas against phlogiston. By the end of the decade, the phlogiston theory was dead.

# Science for the People

ANTOINE LAVOISIER WAS A VERY productive scientist. He wrote over fifty papers for the Academy of Sciences during his life. Still, he did not work at science full time. Most days he performed experiments only between six and eight o'clock in the morning and between seven and ten at night.

He could spend all day in the laboratory just once a week. Madame Lavoisier called that day his "day of happiness." Friends and fellow scientists joined him there, she wrote. So did students, young men eager to learn from him. Scientists from other countries often visited as well. They had lunch, talked, and did experiments. As a thinker, Lavoisier towered over all of them. "You should have seen and heard this man with his precise mind, . . . his high genius . . . illuminating [lighting up] his conversation," said his admiring wife.[1]

## Government Work

During the rest of the week, Lavoisier worked for the government. Some of his work was for the Tax Farm. He traveled through France to see that taxes were collected fairly. Sometimes he was able to change tax rules that were not fair. For instance, he removed a tax that one province had placed only on Jews.

Lavoisier would have liked to make greater changes. He wanted to see nobles pay more taxes and poor people pay less. "If it is allowable to make exceptions in . . . taxes, it can only be in favor of the poor," he wrote.[2] He would have liked to see taxes made the same throughout France, too. The government and the Tax Farm did not want to make these changes, though.

One idea of Lavoisier's that they did accept worked out badly. The Tax Farm was supposed to collect a tax on all goods entering Paris, but sneaking goods into the city without paying was easy. About a fifth of the goods from outside that were sold in Paris had not been taxed. This lost money for the farm. It also hurt the merchants who had paid the tax.

To stop this problem, Lavoisier suggested building a wall around Paris. People would have to enter the city through gates in the wall. Agents at the gates could easily see what everyone carried and tax it.

The government built the wall, starting in 1783. The wall was six feet high and had sixty-six toll gates. Parisians said it made them feel as if they were in jail. They even thought it blocked fresh air and might make them sick. Some said Lavoisier ought to be hanged for thinking of it.

Lavoisier had better luck with another government job, which gained him a new home. In 1775, he and three other men were put in charge of making gunpowder for France. The four were to live in the Paris Arsenal, where the city's gunpowder was stored. Lavoisier was given a luxurious set of rooms there. He and his wife would live in them for seventeen years. One became his laboratory, filled with expensive equipment.

Lavoisier more than earned his fine living quarters. Before 1775, the country's gunpowder had been made by a private company, set up much like the Tax Farm. It made very little powder, and it made it badly. As a result, France had to buy most of its powder from other countries. French soldiers sometimes lost battles because they did not have enough gunpowder. Lavoisier used his skills as a chemist and manager to change that.

Gunpowder was made from sulfur, charcoal, and niter (potassium nitrate). The niter came from a substance called saltpeter. Saltpeter formed on stones in damp places such as cellars and barns. It also appeared in soil near where farm animals were kept. The powder company's agents had the right to go into people's farms and homes to look for it, and they often abused that right. People hated them almost as much as they did the tax collectors.

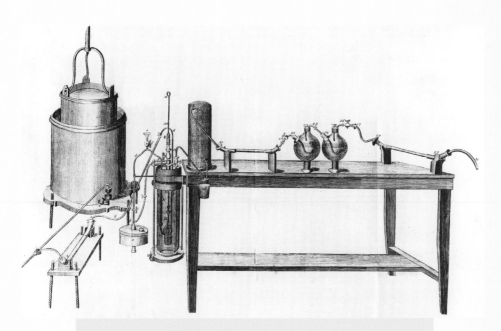

Lavoisier filled his laboratory at the Arsenal with expensive and complex equipment. This setup was used to find out what substances were contained in oil. The oil was burned in the large vessel on the left. The rest of the equipment collected different gases that were given off.

Lavoisier learned that some countries made their own saltpeter. They filled ditches with manure, rotting plants, chalky soil or rocks, and a little water. The ditches were called niter beds. Saltpeter formed there, just as it did in nature, but in larger amounts.

Lavoisier got France to start using niter beds. He made other changes as well. Because of them, the country had all the gunpowder it needed within a few years. It even had enough left over to sell. (Some went to the British colonies in North America. "North America owes its independence to French gunpowder," Lavoisier wrote in 1789.[3]) The quality of the powder was much improved, too. By 1788, the powder could throw a cannonball almost twice as far as in 1775. French powder was then said to be the best in Europe.

## Helping Farmers

Lavoisier helped the French people in peace as well as in war. Since the time he had traveled through the country with Jean Guettard, he had known about the hard lives of French farmers. Part of their problems came from high taxes. Another part, though, came from the way they farmed. As he had done with gunpowder, Lavoisier hoped to use science to improve French farming.

To study farming methods, Lavoisier needed a farm. In 1778 he bought one, a twelve-hundred-acre estate called Fréchines. It became Europe's first experimental farm. Twice a year, Lavoisier stayed there for a month. The rest of the time, a friend ran the estate according to Lavoisier's instructions.

Lavoisier knew that a successful farm needed both plants and animals. Manure from sheep and cattle made good fertilizer. It put nutrients into the soil that crops could use. Crops thus grew better when manure was spread on the fields. The animals, in turn, needed plants for food. Part of a farm's land, Lavoisier said, should be used to grow hay that farm animals could eat in the winter. Then farmers would not have to buy food for them.

Most farmers did not know the importance of manure and hay. Lavoisier used Fréchines to show them. He tried his methods on the poorest land in the estate. Some of it was marshland, which he drained to make meadows where hay could be grown. He had sheep moved from one field to another. This spread their manure around.

Changes on a farm take a long time to show results. By 1793, though, Fréchines was producing more than twice as much wheat as it had when Lavoisier bought it. The estate had five times as many animals.

In 1785, Lavoisier was placed on a Committee for Agriculture (farming). He described his work at Fréchines to this group in 1788. He advised the government to teach farmers his methods.

## Investigating for the Academy

Lavoisier served on many other government committees as well. He also joined many different committees in the Academy of Sciences. Such committees were formed when the government asked the academy to look into certain subjects. Lavoisier wrote or helped to write over two hundred group reports for the academy.

Two of his reports were on the prisons and hospitals of Paris. In 1780, his group found that the city's prisons were dark, damp, and filthy. They were packed with people. Rats, mice, and insects were everywhere. He wrote in 1787 that the hospitals were not much better. Each large bed held five people. People of all ages and both sexes were mixed together, and diseases often passed from one to another. The air smelled terrible. A greater percentage of people died in Paris hospitals than in any others in Europe.

Lavoisier suggested ways to improve the prisons and hospitals. He showed how fresh air and water could be brought in. He described how to keep people and rooms clean. However, no changes were made.

One of the oddest subjects Lavoisier looked into for the academy was a medical treatment called mesmerism. Anton Mesmer, a German-born doctor, had invented it. It had become quite popular, first in America and then in France.

Most people knew about magnetism, which makes compass needles point north. Mesmer said that people had magnetism, too. He called it animal magnetism. He said it could be passed from one person to another.

When people thought they had been "magnetized," they often acted strangely. They might cry out, laugh, or faint. Some had convulsions, or shaking fits. Some sick people said they felt better.

Mesmer said his treatments could cure illness, but French doctors doubted this. They thought mesmerism might even be harmful. In 1784, they asked the Academy of Sciences to find out more about it. The academy gave this task to a committee that included Lavoisier. The American statesman and scientist Benjamin Franklin was living in Paris at the time, and he also joined the committee.

Some people took the mesmerism treatment in groups. The committee went to some of these gatherings, which were like strange parties. Music played in the background. Holding hands, guests sat around a tub full of bottles of water that was supposed to be magnetized.

Iron rods stuck out of the tub. The people

Benjamin Franklin was a scientist as well as a statesman. He lived in Paris for a while and knew Lavoisier. Franklin helped Lavoisier prove that Anton Mesmer's medical treatment was a fake.

sometimes touched these to parts of their bodies that they wanted to heal. Meanwhile, Mesmer's assistant, Deslon, walked through the room. Sometimes Deslon moved a wand over the people's bodies to magnetize them.

The committee brought instruments to the gatherings. Some instruments could detect electricity, while others could spot magnetism. None showed anything special in the water, rods, or wand.

The group also tested people who had fits when they thought they were magnetized. Sometimes the group blindfolded the people. They told them that Deslon was magnetizing them. In fact, Deslon was not there. The people still had fits. At other times, they had the people sit next to a cardboard screen. Behind the screen, Deslon tried to magnetize them. The people did not know this was being done. They showed no response to the treatment.

In 1784 the committee published a report on its tests. Animal magnetism, it said, was not a physical force. If Mesmer's treatment cured illness, it did so only because people believed it would. They were helped not by magnetism but by their own minds.

Most Parisians stopped using the treatment after that. In time, Mesmer left the country. Some of his followers stayed on, though. Some felt that Lavoisier and the other scientists had not treated them fairly. Like the people who disliked the Paris wall, they hoped that someday they would have a chance to punish him.

# 5

# A Revolution in Chemistry

ANTOINE LAVOISIER WAS FORTY-FOUR IN 1787. He had achieved all the success his early life had promised—and then some. Now, though, he wanted to take on a new challenge. It was not enough to have changed the way chemists thought about one important part of chemistry. He wanted to change the way they thought about chemistry itself.

## A New Language for Science

To do that, Lavoisier knew he would have to alter the way scientists *talked* about chemistry. He would have to change the terms and language they used. Much of that language was confusing. Sometimes one compound had several names, for instance. Some names told

Many chemical names came from long ago, when chemists were called alchemists. This picture shows an alchemist seated on the left and his assistants working in the laboratory.

where a substance came from. Others told how it was made. Still others told what it looked like. Some terms used in chemistry reflected ancient beliefs and theories that chemists no longer thought were true.

Lavoisier said that a good naming system should help people understand chemistry. It would also help chemists name new substances and show how these were related to older ones. (Many new substances had been discovered in the 1700s.) He thought that a compound's name should tell what is in it. The name should also give a chemist clues about how to make the compound and how it will react with others.

Lavoisier got the idea of changing chemical names from another French chemist, Guyton de Morveau. He worked out a naming system with de Morveau and two other chemists, and they published a book about it in 1787. Two years later, Lavoisier described the system again in his longest book. In English, this book is called *Elements of Chemistry*.

The new system of chemical names followed a pattern designed to name plants and animals. Carl Linnaeus, a Swedish biologist, had invented this pattern earlier in the century. In it, each kind of living organism has two names. Both are in Latin, an ancient language that all scientists of the time learned.

The first name in Linnaeus's system tells the genus to which a living thing belongs. A genus is a group of closely related organisms. The second name describes the species. For instance, the name for dogs is *Canis familiaris*. *Canis* is the genus name for all dogs, wolves, jackals, and coyotes. *Familiaris* names the species of dog that humans have tamed, or domesticated.

Lavoisier's system of chemical names works almost the same way. This time the "genus name" comes second, though. It is like people's names in English. For instance, one group of compounds is called the acids. *Acid* is the family (genus) name. The "species" name comes from an element in a certain acid. Nitric acid contains nitrogen, for instance.

Two acids can sometimes be made from the same element. Lavoisier put a suffix, or ending, on the "species" name to show the difference. The suffix acts something like a person's middle name. Jo Beth Smith is not the same as Jo Ann Smith. In the same way, nitr*ous* acid is different from nitr*ic* acid. The two contain different amounts of oxygen. Some family names have suffixes, too. The suffix *–ide*, for instance, means that a compound contains just two elements.

## A World-Changing Book

*Elements of Chemistry* contains much more than the new naming system. It sums up Lavoisier's discoveries and theories, which were closely tied to his naming system. He wanted students to use his book to learn chemistry as he saw it.

The word *elements* in the book title means "basic facts." In the book itself, Lavoisier used this same word with two other meanings. One is "the building blocks of matter." Since ancient times, scientists had tried to describe what these might be. (Chemists now use the word *atoms* for these building blocks. This term comes from one of the ancient theories.) Lavoisier was more honest. He wrote, "We know nothing at all about them."[1]

The other meaning of *elements* is "substances that cannot be broken down." Lavoisier's book listed thirty-three of these. He kept the ancient names for most: iron, mercury, and so on. He warned that the list might change. Some substances might turn out to be compounds and would have to be removed. (He did not guess that more elements might be added. That has happened, though.) No one before had admitted that a list of elements might change.

One of the most important ideas in Lavoisier's book is that matter cannot be created or destroyed in chemical reactions. The weight of all substances at the end of a reaction will be the same as the weight of all substances at the start. "Upon this principle," Lavoisier wrote, "the whole art of performing chemical experiments depends."[2] He may have been the first to state this idea.

Because of this rule, chemists can use measurement to discover what happens in reactions. They can also write what happens in the form of an equation. An equation is a statement of equality. An equation in math might say $3 + 5 = 4 + 4$. In the same way, a chemist might write: $2\,H_2 + O_2 \rightarrow 2\,H_2O$. This statement shows how water is formed from hydrogen and oxygen. (One or two letters stand for the name of each element in an equation. In this equation, $H$ stands for hydrogen, and $O$ stands for oxygen.)

The first part of Lavoisier's book described his ideas about heat. It also told about air and other gases. He was one of the first scientists to say that matter can exist in three states: solid, liquid, and gas. Changing the amount of heat energy in a substance can change its state. Adding a certain amount of heat to a solid changes it into a liquid, as when heated ice melts to make liquid water. If enough heat is added, the liquid boils and becomes a gas. This section of the book explained Lavoisier's system of chemical names as well.

The second part of Lavoisier's book described the major chemical families, including compounds from living things. Most of these had never been broken down into their elements. Lavoisier showed that compounds from plants contained hydrogen, oxygen, and carbon. Those from animals most often contained nitrogen as well. These studies were some of the first in what was later called organic chemistry.

The third part of *Elements of Chemistry* described instruments used in this science and told how they worked. Lavoisier had most of these instruments in his laboratory. Madame Lavoisier drew pictures of some of them for the book.

*Elements of Chemistry* was Antoine Lavoisier's masterpiece. It gave a completely new view of chemistry. Chemists still use that view today.

Some older chemists, including Priestley and Cavendish, never accepted the ideas in Lavoisier's book. Most chemists, though, liked the new naming system. In using the names, they accepted Lavoisier's oxygen theory. Two years after *Elements of Chemistry* was published, Lavoisier wrote, "All the young adopt the new theory, which tells me that the revolution in chemistry is over."[3]

Meanwhile, though, a deadlier revolution had begun.

# 6

# A Deadlier Revolution

BY 1788, FRANCE WAS BROKE. FOR MANY years its government had spent too much money. Wars had used some of it. The king and queen had spent much on their costly court. Now there was nothing to spend. The middle class refused to pay more taxes, and the poor had nothing to pay with. Many could not even buy food.

The desperate king, Louis XVI, finally agreed to do something that had not been done for 175 years. He would call the Estates-General. This lawmaking body was a little like the British Parliament or the United States Congress.

Louis and his nobles hoped that the Estates-General would help them find new ways to obtain money. The people of France hoped that the lawmakers would cut taxes and limit the power of the king and government. Neither party got its wish.

The Estates-General met on May 5, 1789, at the king's palace in Versailles. The lawmakers refused to do what Louis wanted, and he tried to break up the group. The members of the Estates-General, however, would not go home. On June 17 they changed their body's name to the National Assembly. They said it would make all future laws. They swore to stay together and write a constitution for France.

## The Revolution Begins

That was the beginning of great changes. In July, the people of Paris heard rumors that the king planned to send soldiers to the city. They took steps to defend themselves. First, they formed a city government called a commune. They started to tear down Lavoisier's hated wall. Then, on July 14, they took over the grim city fortress called the Bastille.

At the same time, peasants in the countryside attacked nobles' castles. Sometimes they burned

The French Revolution began on July 14, 1789, when an angry mob of Parisians took over a fortress called the Bastille.

the castles and killed their occupants. Many nobles fled the country. They could see that a full-scale revolution had begun.

Lavoisier barely escaped the Paris mob. On August 6, a large load of gunpowder was taken out of the Arsenal and put on a river barge to be carried to a distant town. It was supposed to be used by traders in Africa. In French, as in English, however, the words for *trader* and *traitor* sound almost alike. A rumor began to spread that the powder was going to the "traitors" who opposed the revolution.

Confusing orders from different officials made things worse. The barge was unloaded, loaded, and unloaded again. A mob threatened to attack the Arsenal and kill the powder commissioners. Lavoisier finally explained everything to the Paris leaders, but many people still believed he had plotted against the revolution.

By the start of 1790, Lavoisier was growing nervous. Still, he hoped that in the long run, the revolution would help France. He wanted the country to have a constitutional monarchy like Britain's. In such a system, the king would still head the state, but most government power would belong to the National Assembly. That group would represent the people.

At this time, Lavoisier still thought such a plan was possible. He knew that most members of the assembly were educated, law-abiding men of the middle or upper middle classes. They were guided by reason and had the people's good (as they saw it) at heart. In short, they were like him. Most wanted the same kind of government he did.

On March 10, the assembly gave Lavoisier a very important job. They asked him and other scientists to set up standard weights and measures for the country. At the time, different parts of France used different measures. Having standards that all could agree on would help trade within France. It would also help the French to trade with other countries.

The weights and measures that Lavoisier's group established became the metric system, which is used in most of the world today. Lavoisier's particular task in the weights and measures committee was to find the weight of a cubic centimeter (0.06 cubic inches) of pure water in a vacuum at 0° C (32° F). This became the standard for the unit called the gram.

## Human Respiration

At the same time, Lavoisier was trying to do his own science. He was now studying human respiration. A young chemist named Armand Séguin was the "guinea pig" in the tests. He did not have to sit surrounded by ice, like the guinea pig in the calorimeter. Instead, he breathed oxygen through a tube in an air-proof mask. Lavoisier measured how much gas Séguin used. He also measured the speed of Séguin's breathing and heartbeat (pulse). The faster Séguin's heart beat, the faster blood moved through his body.

Lavoisier tested Séguin when Séguin was sitting still. He did it again while Séguin pressed a foot pedal that lifted a weight. He did it before and after Séguin ate. Madame Lavoisier made drawings of these experiments.

Lavoisier found that Séguin used almost three times as much oxygen while working as while resting. His breathing and pulse were faster, too. Noting that respiration speeded up during work was an important discovery.

Lavoisier studied human respiration with the help of a young chemist named Armand Séguin. Séguin, on the far left, is breathing through an air-proof mask. Lavoisier is second from the right. Madame Lavoisier, who drew this picture, is on the far right.

Séguin used extra oxygen while digesting food, although the amount was not nearly as great as the amount he used while working. He also used up more oxygen on cold days than on warm ones. This supported Lavoisier's belief that heat from respiration warmed the body.

Lavoisier described his work to the Academy of Sciences late in 1790. He had said before that

In this picture, Séguin is exercising by working a foot pedal that lifts a weight. Lavoisier (second from left) showed that Séguin used more oxygen when exercising than when resting, as in the previous picture.

respiration was a combustion. Now he said that the fuel it burned came from food. Food was like the oil burned in a lamp. "If the animal did not receive . . . from food what it loses by respiration, the lamps would soon run short of oil," he said. "The animal [would] perish [die], as a lamp goes out when its fuel is exhausted."[1]

## Darkening Times

Some of France's new leaders were not impressed with Lavoisier or his science. One was Jean-Paul Marat. Marat had once hoped to be known as a scientist. In 1780, he had published a theory of burning, and Lavoisier had reviewed it for the Academy of Sciences. Lavoisier said that Marat's theory was nonsense.

Marat had never forgiven the academy—or Lavoisier. In 1791 he attacked them in his newspaper, *The Friend of the People*, and in other writings. He said Lavoisier was "the putative [supposed] father of all the discoveries which are noised abroad [talked about] . . . he has no ideas of his own [so] he appropriates [steals] those of others . . . he abandons them as lightly as he adopts them, and he changes his systems as he does his shoes. . . . He rests on his laurels [gets by on his reputation] while his disciples [followers] praise him to the skies."[2]

Some readers would later remember Marat's rantings. Lavoisier was too busy to pay them much mind, though. He was making a kind of

Jean-Paul Marat, like many other leaders of the French Revolution, distrusted scientists. Some of Marat's writings made fun of Lavoisier and called him a fake.

economic census of France. He gave this report to the National Assembly on March 15, 1791. It listed France's population and the average wealth per person. It showed the amounts of different farm and factory products made each year. In effect, it described what would now be called the country's gross national product. Such a report had never been made before in France. Lavoisier said a government had to know these kinds of facts. Without them, it could not plan wisely for the country's economy.

Meanwhile, the National Assembly began to look at the hated Tax Farm. People accused the Farmers-General of keeping money that should have gone to the government. They asked the assembly to examine the tax farmers' papers and seize all their wealth.

On March 20, 1791, the National Assembly ruled that the Tax Farm would no longer exist. It assigned six Farmers-General to draw up an account of the Tax Farm's finances. Lavoisier was not one of them.

Lavoisier himself was still in favor. In April,

the Assembly chose him and five other men to control the National Treasury. He took the post without salary, saying that the pay from his gunpowder job was enough for him. He hoped to keep the gunpowder post because he did not want to lose his home and laboratory in the Arsenal.

On October 1, the National Assembly finished the country's constitution and held new elections. It said that no one who had been in the old assembly could be in the new one. That meant that most of the new members had no experience in government. Many of them also had little education. These new leaders wanted reforms far beyond what was in the constitution. "The present constitution has no friends and cannot last," the British ambassador wrote.[3]

Lavoisier tried to work with the new assembly. Early in 1792, he made a long report to them, describing the country's finances as of January 1. The report presented a grim picture.

In the same month, the assembly made Lavoisier a member of the Advisory Board of

Arts and Crafts. This group was supposed to advise the government about inventions. It came to cover much more, though, including education.

Lavoisier realized that even he could not handle so many jobs at once, so he gave up his treasury post. Indeed, he now tried to avoid all paid government jobs. More and more, he disliked and feared the assembly leaders. He was loyal to the constitution, the king, and reason. He felt that they cared for none of these things.

In late April 1792, Antoine Fourcroy, a chemist who had sometimes worked with Lavoisier, said that the Academy of Sciences should drop members who had left the country. It should also drop those who might not support the revolution. The academy had never taken sides in politics, though, and it refused to do so now. It agreed only to send a list of its members to the assembly. The assembly could remove names from the list if it wanted to.

In August, a mob again swept through Paris. It set up a new city government. This government was as strong as the assembly. It all but ruled the country.

Such a mob had endangered Lavoisier before, and he feared it would do so again. Sadly, he gave up his gunpowder job, his laboratory, and his home. He and his wife left the Arsenal on August 15. They escaped just in time. Three days later, police came to the Arsenal and tried to arrest all the powder commissioners.

In September, the Paris mob yanked most political prisoners out of jail. They killed fourteen hundred of them after one-minute trials. Lavoisier was not there to see the slaughter. He and Marie had gone to Fréchines.

Lavoisier had always been kind to the people at Fréchines. If he had stayed there, he might have been safe. When the Academy of Sciences met again in November, though, he went back to Paris. He would never have a chance to leave the capital again.

# "Only a Moment . . ."

IN SEPTEMBER 1792, FRANCE CHOSE YET another lawmaking body. It called itself the National Convention. This group tried to change everything about the country.

To start with, the convention made France a republic. It said that representatives of the people, not kings, would rule from then on. It started the country's calendar over from the first day of the republic—September 22, 1792. It even gave the months new names. The names described the weather at different times of year.

## A Time of Executions

Convention leaders wanted all traces of the old ways wiped out. They felt the same about all who had been part of the old ruling class. Executions after brief trials became common. King Louis XVI was one of the first to go. A new device called the guillotine cut off his head on January 23, 1793. The queen, Marie Antoinette, was executed in the same way on October 16.

Organizations, too, "went under the knife." Most convention leaders did not trust highly educated people. Learned academies, they thought, were too much like the old groups of nobles. These

**King Louis XVI and his wasteful court brought France to the edge of ruin. He was executed during the French Revolution.**

leaders wanted all the academies broken up, including the Academy of Sciences.

Lavoisier had belonged to the academy for twenty-four years. He had been its director in 1785 and became its treasurer at the end of 1791. Many of its members were his friends.

Fighting the convention was risky, but when the academy was attacked, Lavoisier defended it. One biographer wrote that he became "the very soul of the dying Academy."[1]

In speech after speech, Lavoisier tried to show the convention how important the academy was. He explained why scientists needed to share their research. He reminded the group that the academy did work that the convention valued. It had handled the weights and measures program, for instance. None of this did any good. On August 8, 1793, the convention closed down all learned societies.

Meanwhile, the National Convention was also criticizing the other group that had shaped Lavoisier's life. The complex accounts of the Tax Farm still were not finished. Convention leaders began complaining that the farmers were delaying on purpose.

Many leaders still thought the farmers were hiding stolen money. In September, they ordered the homes of all the former Farmers-General searched. The police found no sign of wrongdoing in Lavoisier's new Paris home. An official wrote to him, "Everything there pays homage to your loyalty and removes all suspicion."[2]

On September 26, a new group began to check the accounts of the Tax Farm. A man named Antoine Dupin was in charge. He said he had found proof that the farmers were criminals. Taking his word, on November 24 the National Convention ordered all the tax farmers arrested. Their property was seized as well.

In those days, an arrest meant almost sure death. Lavoisier hoped to delay his arrest until he could prepare a good defense. He therefore looked for a place to hide. At last he thought of the building where the Academy of Sciences had met. He found an old servant who let him in.

For four days, Lavoisier hid in a dusty meeting room, writing letters. None had any effect. France's new rulers did not care about his fame as a scientist. They did not care about his work on weights and measures or other government projects. He was rich, educated, and a nobleman of sorts. Worst of all, he had been a tax farmer. That was all that mattered.

## Sent to Prison

Lavoisier feared that the servant who had helped him would suffer if he were caught in his hiding place. To prevent that, he gave himself up on November 28. Like his father-in-law Jacques Paulze and thirty-one other tax farmers, he was sent to prison.

Conditions at the prison were not too bad. Guards stood at the outer doors, but the men were not locked into their cells. Lavoisier had a large cell with a fireplace, which he shared with Paulze and one other man. Because it was better than most other cells, the other farmers began using it as a meeting room.

In spite of their talk, Lavoisier settled down to work. He had made plans for an eight-volume book on chemistry. The book would also tell about his life. During his time in prison he managed to write two of the volumes.

Marie came to see him, of course. She was

This painting of Lavoisier's arrest shows a dramatic event that never happened. Instead of being arrested in his laboratory, Lavoisier actually gave himself up.

doing her best to get him freed. After one of her visits, Lavoisier wrote her this letter:

> You give yourself, sweetheart, a lot of trouble and much weariness of mind and body, and I cannot share it. Be careful lest you impair [damage] your health. . . . I am getting on in years, my life has been a happy one for as far back as I remember, you . . .

contribute to it every day by the marks of affection that you show me. . . . My task is finished, but you may expect to have a long life . . . do not squander it [throw it away]. I thought I noticed yesterday that you were sad; why should you be since I am quite resigned. . . . However, we are not without hope of being reunited.[3]

The National Convention realized at last that the tax farmers could not do their accounts if they could not get at their papers. Therefore, it turned the old Tax Farm offices into a jail and moved the farmers there.

The accounts were finally finished on January 27, 1794. The tax farmers hoped that now they would be set free. All that happened, though, was that the many charges against them were boiled down to three: They had stolen a huge sum of money from the government. They had charged too high an interest rate on their loans. Finally, they had put too much water in the tobacco they sold. (Merchants who sold tobacco had to buy it from the Tax Farm.) This supposedly not only cheated the people but harmed their health.

Lavoisier prepared a defense for the tax farmers. He showed their innocence of each charge. He also wrote up a defense for himself.

He might as well not have bothered. The revolution was now in the stage called the Reign of Terror. The National Convention had passed a law saying that people even suspected of opposing the republic could be jailed. Trials were swift, and verdicts were almost always "guilty." The punishment was death. Sometimes over two hundred and fifty people were tried and executed in one day. Among those put to death were some of the first leaders of the revolution.

Some groups Lavoisier had served with asked for his release. Many of his old friends, though, were strangely silent. At least two, Guyton and Fourcroy, were on important government committees. Their pleas might have worked—yet they said nothing. Most likely they were afraid to speak. Jealousy may also have kept them quiet, however. With Lavoisier out of the way, their chance for fame as chemists would be greater.

## Condemned to Die

On May 5, Dupin talked the National Convention into having the tax farmers put on trial by the Revolutionary Tribunal. Most of the death sentences came from this special court. It was supposed to try only those accused of crimes against the republic, and the tax farmers' supposed crimes had taken place before the republic existed. That did not stop those who wanted their death, though. They said that the farmers had weakened the country. This was counted as a crime against the republic, even though it had happened earlier.

The farmers were taken to a grimmer prison, the Conciergerie, that same night. They spent two unhappy days there before their trial. Most had no blankets. Some had no beds. During this time Lavoisier wrote to a cousin, "I have had a fairly long career, and above all, a happy one and I believe that my memory will be accompanied by some regrets, perhaps by some glory. What more could one wish? This affair will probably save me the inconvenience of old age. I shall die in good health."[4]

These were brave words. In another part of his letter, though, Lavoisier showed his anger: "Social virtues, important services to country, a useful life employed in the interests of the arts and human knowledge cannot preserve me from this dismal end; I must perish as a guilty person."[5] This letter is thought to be Lavoisier's last.

The tax farmers were tried together by the Revolutionary Tribunal on May 8. The trial was a joke. The men had just fifteen minutes to talk with their defense lawyers, whom they had never met before. But what did it matter? There was no doubt what the verdict would be.

The chief judge was a large young man with a loud voice. He was fittingly named Coffinhal. During the trial, a brave member of the Board of Arts and Crafts read a speech pointing out Lavoisier's importance as a scientist. Coffinhal is said to have snapped, "The Republic has no need for scientists."[6]

As expected, the jury found all the men guilty. Coffinhal sentenced them to die. When they got back to their prison, the heavy carts that hauled prisoners to their execution were waiting. In late afternoon, the men rode to the open square where the guillotine stood.

One by one the tax farmers knelt before the big blade. Paulze was the third to die. Lavoisier was fourth. When the butchery was done, the bodies were buried in a mass grave. The next day, the mathematician Joseph Lagrange told a friend, "It required only a moment to sever [cut off] his [Lavoisier's] head, and probably one hundred years will not suffice [be enough] to produce another like it."[7]

Marie Lavoisier was left with nothing. Her husband and father were dead. The government had seized her home, money, and goods. She was even sent to prison for two months in the summer, though there were no charges against her. After her release, an old servant gave her a place to live.

The only things Madame Lavoisier had left

were her spirit—and time. The Terror claimed many innocent lives, and most French people grew sick of it. The leader of the Terror, Maximilien Robespierre, was overthrown in late July. He then took his own turn under the guillotine.

Heartened by the changing times, Madame Lavoisier fought back. In December 1794, she led the families of the other tax farmers in asking to have some of their possessions returned. By the summer of 1795 she had regained most of her family's money. She even got Lavoisier's expensive lab instruments back. By then, documents called her the "widow of the unjustly condemned Lavoisier."[8] A new review of the tax farmers' accounts had shown that the government had owed the farm money, not the other way around.

The wounds of Madame Lavoisier's private loss took longer to heal. In 1805, though, she again began to entertain scientists in her home. The revolution was long over by then. The Academy of Sciences had been restored. France was an empire, run by a new leader named Napoleon.

One scientist who visited Madame Lavoisier was an American, Benjamin Thompson. He was famous for his work on heat. He now lived in Europe and had even won a noble title, Count Rumford. He and Madame Lavoisier married on October 22, 1805. Unlike Marie's marriage to Lavoisier, this did not prove to be a happy one. The pair divorced in 1809.

Marie Lavoisier lived on in Paris for many years afterward. She died on February 10, 1836—forty-two years after the husband she had loved so much.

# 8

# Founder of Modern Chemistry

IN 1869, ABOUT A HUNDRED YEARS AFTER Antoine Lavoisier began making his discoveries, a Frenchman named Adolph Wurtz wrote a short history of chemistry. In it he said, "Chemistry is a French science; it was founded by Lavoisier of immortal fame."[1] At that time, each nation in Europe loudly praised its own achievements. Wurtz's statement surely was an exaggeration—but it may not have been completely wrong.

## Strengths and Weaknesses

Lavoisier sometimes exaggerated his own achievements. He often did not give credit to the scientists upon whose work he built. For instance, when he wrote how he had found "pure air" by breaking down mercury calx, he did not say that Joseph Priestley had given him the idea for this experiment. In the same way, he did not say that the idea for the experiment showing how water was made came from Blagden and Cavendish. Both Priestley and Blagden protested this treatment.

Lavoisier may have neglected other scientists, but he made sure that no one did the same to him. When his theory of combustion became widely known, some people called it "the theory of the French chemists." He wrote angrily, "This theory is not . . . the theory of the French chemists, it is *mine*."[2]

Lavoisier always stressed the importance of weighing and measuring. Without them, he said, "neither physics nor chemistry can . . . admit anything whatsoever."[3] He spent much money on fine balances and other measuring tools. For all his care, though, some historians of science say he was not as good an experimenter as Priestley or Cavendish. He sometimes claimed his results were more exact than they were. He sometimes changed his measurements to make them fit his theories.

Lavoisier's greatest skill was not in designing or doing experiments, but in realizing what experiments *meant*. Once, when someone complained that he had claimed credit for work that was not his, he wrote, "It will at least not be disputed that the conclusions [in my book] are my own."[4] They certainly were. Priestley found oxygen first, but Lavoisier was the one who showed how this gas worked in burning and breathing. Cavendish showed that burning hydrogen and oxygen together made water, but only Lavoisier recognized that water was a compound of the two gases. It is for his conclusions that Lavoisier will always be remembered.

He will also be remembered for the way he organized those conclusions. Builders combine stones to make a fine house. In the same way, Lavoisier combined facts to make a new system of chemistry. Much has changed in chemistry since his time, but chemists still use his names and his way of describing reactions.

## Building on Lavoisier's Foundations

A house may be remodeled over the years. A new room or set of rooms may be added. In the same way, later chemists built on Lavoisier's work. They changed his list of elements, for instance. Some elements turned out to be compounds after all, and they were taken off the list. Others were added.

Other scientists built on what Lavoisier learned about compounds from living things. He had found that these complex compounds were made of just a few elements. By about sixty years later, chemists were learning how these substances were put together. They founded the science of organic chemistry.

Still others studied the chemical processes in living things. ("La vie est une function chemique," Lavoisier once wrote, which means, "Life is a function of chemistry."[5]) They found out more about respiration. They learned how blood carries oxygen to the muscles. Much of the "burning" of respiration takes place there, not in the lungs as Lavoisier had thought. (Some respiration takes place in all cells, but respiration is especially important in giving muscles the energy they need for moving.) Respiration is a more complex process than Lavoisier thought, but his basic understanding of it was right.

Finally, Lavoisier should be remembered for the ways he tried to help the French people. It was not his fault that neither France's old government nor its new one listened to him. Some of his ideas were eventually used. He said that a country's government should pay to send all children to school, for example. He said it should help people save money for their old age. Many governments do these things today.

In 1789, Lavoisier wrote: "It is not . . . necessary in order to deserve well of mankind . . . to be called to glittering public office. . . . The man of science in the silence of his laboratory . . . can also serve his country: by

A hundred years after Lavoisier's death, the French government put up this statue in Paris to honor him. The monument recognized that he had greatly advanced science and tried to help the French people.

his work . . . he may diminish . . . the evils that afflict the human race."[6]

Antoine Lavoisier served his country in both public office and laboratory. He studied government budgets and chemical reactions with the same clear mind. He used science to help people make weapons of war and grow food in peacetime. In his short but amazingly productive life, he served not only France but humanity as well.

# Afterword:
# Very Small Chemistry

ANTOINE LAVOISIER UNDERSTOOD perhaps more about chemistry than anyone before him. Still, he did not live long enough to learn about atoms and molecules, the building blocks that take part in chemical reactions. Scientists began to talk about these particles in the early nineteenth century. (Marie Lavoisier probably heard about them.) Each chemical element has its own kind of atom. A molecule is made of two or more atoms held together by chemical forces, or bonds. In a chemical reaction, atoms move from one molecule to another. As a result, molecules are broken down, rearranged, or combined.

Today, some scientists are learning how to control atoms and molecules in a new way. Someday they may be able to move single atoms or molecules from place to place. They may build machines too small to see without a microscope. Their field is called nanotechnology. Nanotechnology deals with particles between one and one hundred nanometers long, called nanoparticles. A nanometer is a billionth of a meter, or 0.00000004 inch. Only three or four atoms will fit in a nanometer. A human hair is about twenty-five thousand nanometers wide.

Nanotechnology combines chemistry, physics, engineering, and sometimes, even biology. The rules of all these sciences change in the nano realm. A news Web site called *Nanotechnology Now* explains why: "Things are different at different size scales. A flea can jump many times its height; an elephant cannot jump at all. In general, smaller things move faster, weigh less, and are often more powerful. . . . Sometimes, very small things behave differently [from larger ones] because of physics quirks . . . called 'quantum effects.'"[1]

Nanoparticles also have more surface area in the same amount of mass (weight) than larger particles. In solids, chemical reactions most often take place on surfaces. Because of this, nanoparticles react more easily and strongly.

Physicist Richard Feynman, who later won a Nobel Prize, suggested the basic idea of nanotechnology in 1959. In a speech called "There's Plenty of Room at the Bottom," he said, "The principles of physics, as far as I can see, do not speak against the possibility of maneuvering [placing and moving] things atom by atom."[2]

In the late 1970s, another scientist, Eric Drexler, began saying that nanotechnology might be used to make products. Drexler described his ideas in a book called *Engines of Creation*, published in 1986. This book brought the term *nanotechnology* to English-speaking readers. (A Japanese scientist had used it earlier.)

## Kinds of Nanotechnology

One kind of nanotechnology makes products that include nanoparticles. It is called nanoscale technology. People can already buy such products. Clear sunscreen lotions contain nanoparticles, for instance. Nanoparticles of silver can kill disease-causing bacteria. They are used in some food containers, shoe liners, bandages, and soaps.

Companies are working to develop more products like these. For example, the car manufacturer Toyota has made car bumpers out of a plastic containing nanoparticles. The bumpers weighed 60 percent less than regular ones. They also resisted scratching and denting twice as well.

The most exciting nanotechnology has not been created yet, however. It is called molecular manufacturing. In *Engines of Creation*, Eric Drexler described how it might work. This technology would use computer programs to control chemical reactions very precisely. The reactions would build products by putting atoms and molecules together. In the far future, tiny robots (nanobots) might do the manufacturing. They could even make more robots like themselves.

Some scientists think that molecular manufacturing will begin to be used in the decade starting in 2010. Others think it will take much longer. Some think it will never be possible, or at least practical, at all. Drexler and others say, though, that cells in living bodies already carry out a form of molecular manufacturing. The cells use it to make proteins, the chemicals that do most of the work in the body. Substances in the cells called DNA and RNA carry the "computer code" that directs the manufacture. Scientists are learning how to rewrite this code to make substances they want.

## Promise and Danger

If molecular manufacturing does happen, it could bring many good things. It could make computers many times faster than those of today. It could build sensors that spot disease or pollution more accurately than they do now. Nanobot "doctors" might even go inside cells to stop a cancer or repair a heart.

Products could cost much less to make with molecular manufacturing. Nanofactories would need less energy and materials than factories of today. Some writers predict that someday, each person will own a desktop-sized "personal nanofactory." This machine could make anything the person wants.

Any tool can be used for either good or harm. At the time of the French Revolution, the guillotine was a new device. Its inventor wanted to make executions less painful. The leaders of the revolution, though, used it to kill innocent people such as Lavoisier. In the same way, terrorists of the future could use molecular manufacturing to make new weapons. Governments might use nanosensors to spy on people. They might also fight wars to control this powerful technology.

Some people are afraid that the technology itself could be dangerous. They point out that in air pollution, small particles harm health more than large ones. They fear that nanoparticles might make people sick or damage the environment. This could be true even if larger particles of the same materials are harmless.

Critics think that until scientists find out

whether nanoparticles are safe, governments should limit the ways the particles are used. The U.S. Environmental Protection Agency (EPA) said in late 2006 that it will regulate products containing germ-killing nanoparticles.

Molecular manufacturing could be far more dangerous than nanoparticles. Some writers have suggested that nanobots might run out of control. They might turn all matter into what has been called "gray goo." Supporters of nanotechnology say that this is very unlikely to happen. Nanobots could be made without giving them the power to copy themselves.

If Antoine Lavoisier could have known about nanotechnology, he probably would have been excited. He would have hoped that it could bring food and medicine to poor people. But he might have worried, too, about how it would be used. He learned better than anyone what can happen when people do not value reason or when they misuse science.

# Activities

Like Antoine Lavoisier, you can do experiments to explore chemistry. Do these activities. Then try to answer the questions that follow.

## A New Kind of Air

*Materials needed:*

- chalk or baking soda
- vinegar in a cup
- wide-mouthed jar
- candle and match for lighting

*Procedure:*

Have an adult light the candle. Keep it nearby. Drop some chalk or baking soda in the cup of vinegar and hold the open, empty jar upside down over the mixture to catch the gas that comes off. Then, keeping the jar upside down, move it quickly to the candle. Lower it over the burning candle.

*Questions:*

What kind of gas is given off when the chalk or baking soda combines with the vinegar? How does that gas affect a burning candle? Why does it have that effect?

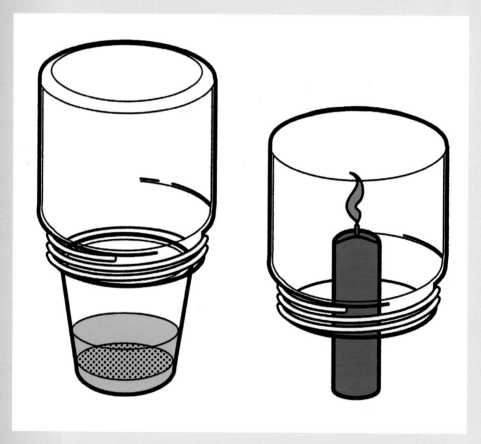

**After filling the jar with gas, place the jar over a candle. What happens to the candle?**

# Rusting Away

*Materials needed:*

- three nails or other small pieces of iron
- dish of water
- sensitive scale if available

*Procedure:*

If you have a sensitive scale, weigh each piece of iron. (If they are all the same, you only need to weigh one of them.) Write down the weight. Put one piece of iron in the dish of water. Wet another piece and leave it in the open, next to the dish. Leave the third piece in the open without wetting it.

Set all the materials outside. Leave them for a month. Check on them every few days and write down any changes you see. At the end of the month, weigh each piece again and write down the weight.

*Questions:*

Which piece of iron rusts most quickly? Which gains the most weight? Where does the extra weight come from? Do you see any bubbles on the iron rusting in the dish of water? If so, what gases do you think the bubbles are, and where do they come from?

## Respiration

*Materials needed:*

- watch or clock that can measure seconds
- pencil and paper

*Procedure:*

Sit quietly and breathe normally. Count the number of breaths you take in exactly one minute. Then find a spot on your wrist where you can feel your pulse (heartbeat). Count the number of heartbeats in one minute. Write these figures down. Now run in place or do some other form of exercise for three minutes. Count your breaths and your pulse for one minute again just after you stop exercising.

*Questions:*

How do your breathing and pulse change after you exercise? Why do you think they change? What substance is your body trying to get more of?

# Chronology

**1743**—Antoine Laurent Lavoisier is born on August 26 in Paris, France.

**1765**—Lavoisier submits first research paper to Academy of Sciences.

**1768**—Lavoisier elected to Academy of Sciences.

**1771**—Lavoisier marries Marie Anne Paulze.

**1773**—Lavoisier plans experiments on air that will "bring about a revolution . . . in chemistry."

**1775**—Lavoisier confirms Joseph Priestley's report that mercury calx gives off "pure air" when broken down.

**1782–1784**—Lavoisier and Simon Laplace do experiments with calorimeter to measure guinea pig's body heat and respiration.

**1783**—Lavoisier reports that water is a compound of hydrogen and oxygen.

**1784**—Lavoisier and Academy of Sciences committee debunk mesmerism.

**1785**—Lavoisier is elected director of the Academy of Sciences.

Lavoisier attacks Stahl's phlogiston theory.

**1787**—Lavoisier and three other chemists describe new system of chemical names.

**1788**—Lavoisier describes experimental farming at Fréchines.

**1789**—*Elements of Chemistry* published.

Estates-General meets; National Assembly formed.

French Revolution begins with takeover of Bastille.

**1790**—Lavoisier and Séguin do experiments on human respiration.

**1791**—Metric system of weights and measures adopted.

Lavoisier presents report on territorial wealth of France to National Assembly.

Tax Farm broken up.

**1792**—Lavoisier gives up gunpowder job and moves out of Arsenal.

France declared a republic.

**1793**—King Louis XVI executed.

Academy of Sciences disbanded.

Farmers-General, including Antoine Lavoisier, arrested.

**1794**—Farmers-General, including Lavoisier, tried, found guilty, and executed on May 8.

**1836**—Madame Lavoisier dies.

# Chapter Notes

### Introduction: Recipes for Revolution

1. Douglas McKie, *Antoine Lavoisier: Scientist, Economist, Social Reformer* (New York: Henry Schuman, 1952), p. 104.

### Chapter 1. Set for Success

1. Douglas McKie, *Antoine Lavoisier: Scientist, Economist, Social Reformer* (New York: Henry Schuman, 1952), p. 131.

2. Arthur Donovan, *Antoine Lavoisier: Science, Administration, and Revolution* (New York: Cambridge University Press, 1996), p. 47.

3. Antoine Lavoisier, *Elements of Chemistry*, translated by Robert Kerr (originally published 1790; reprint New York: Dover Publications, Inc., 1965), p. xviii.

4. Donovan, p. 111.

5. Arthur Young, quoted in W. R. Aykroyd, *Three Philosophers* (Westport, Conn.: Greenwood Press, 1970), p. 88.

### Chapter 2. Fire and Air

1. Douglas McKie, *Antoine Lavoisier: Scientist, Economist, Social Reformer* (New York: Henry Schuman, 1952), p. 104.

2. W.R. Aykroyd, *Three Philosophers* (Westport, Conn.: Greenwood Press, 1970), p. 49.

3. Sidney J. French, *Torch and Crucible: The Life and*

*Death of Antoine Lavoisier* (Princeton, N.J.: Princeton University Press, 1941), p. 89.

4. Ibid.

5. Aykroyd, p. 64.

6. Antoine Lavoisier, *Elements of Chemistry*, translated by Robert Kerr (originally published 1790; reprint New York: Dover Publications, Inc., 1965), p. 36.

7. J.A. Cochrane, *Lavoisier* (London: Constable & Co., Ltd., 1931), p. 59.

8. Ibid., p. 60.

9. McKie, p. 118.

10. Frederic Lawrence Holmes, *Lavoisier and the Chemistry of Life* (Madison, Wisc.: University of Wisconsin Press, 1985), p. 106.

## Chapter 3. Down with Phlogiston

1. Arthur Donovan, *Antoine Lavoisier: Science, Administration, and Revolution* (New York: Cambridge University Press, 1996), p. 169.

2. Frederic Lawrence Holmes, *Lavoisier and the Chemistry of Life* (Madison, Wisc.: University of Wisconsin Press, 1985), p. 193.

3. Douglas McKie, *Antoine Lavoisier: Scientist, Economist, Social Reformer* (New York: Henry Schuman, 1952), p. 148.

4. William H. Brock, *The Norton History of Chemistry* (New York: W. W. Norton & Co., 1993), pp. 111–112.

5. McKie, p. 157.

6. McKie, p. 158.

7. Donovan, p. 173.

## Chapter 4. Science for the People

1. Douglas McKie, *Antoine Lavoisier: Scientist,*

*Economist, Social Reformer* (New York: Henry Schuman, 1952), p. 256.

2. Ibid., p. 257.

3. Arthur Donovan, *Antoine Lavoisier: Science, Administration, and Revolution* (New York: Cambridge University Press, 1996), p. 199.

## Chapter 5. A Revolution in Chemistry

1. Antoine Lavoisier, *Elements of Chemistry*, translated by Robert Kerr (originally published 1790; reprint New York: Dover Publications, Inc., 1965), p. xxiv.

2. Ibid., pp. 130–131.

3. Arthur Donovan, *Antoine Lavoisier: Science, Administration, and Revolution* (New York: Cambridge University Press, 1996), p. 185.

## Chapter 6. A Deadlier Revolution

1. W.R. Aykroyd, *Three Philosophers* (Westport, Conn.: Greenwood Press, 1970), p. 108.

2. J.A. Cochrane, *Lavoisier* (London: Constable & Co., Ltd., 1931), pp. 179–180.

3. Arthur Donovan, *Antoine Lavoisier: Science, Administration, and Revolution* (New York: Cambridge University Press, 1996), p. 264.

## Chapter 7. "Only a Moment . . ."

1. Grimaux, quoted in Douglas McKie, *Antoine Lavoisier: Scientist, Economist, Social Reformer* (New York: Henry Schuman, 1952), p. 356.

2. Piques, quoted in Sidney J. French, *Torch and Crucible: The Life and Death of Antoine Lavoisier* (Princeton, N.J.: Princeton University Press, 1941), p. 242.

3. J.A. Cochrane, *Lavoisier* (London: Constable & Co., Ltd., 1931), p. 228.

4. French, p. 252.

5. Ibid., p. 253.

6. Ibid., p. 255.

7. William H. Brock, *The Norton History of Chemistry* (New York: W. W. Norton & Co., 1993), p. 123.

8. McKie, p. 425.

## Chapter 8. Founder of Modern Chemistry

1. William H. Brock, *The Norton History of Chemistry* (New York: W. W. Norton & Co., 1993), p. 87.

2. Arthur Donovan, *Antoine Lavoisier: Science, Administration, and Revolution* (New York: Cambridge University Press, 1996), p. 182.

3. Brock, p. 117.

4. Douglas McKie, *Antoine Lavoisier: Scientist, Economist, Social Reformer* (New York: Henry Schuman, 1952), p. 170.

5. W. R. Aykroyd, *Three Philosophers* (Westport, Conn.: Greenwood Press, 1970), p. 112.

6. McKie, p. 352.

## Afterword: Very Small Chemistry

1. *Nanotechnology Now* Press Kit, "Introduction to Nanoscale Technology." <http://www.nanotech-now.com/Press_Kit/nanotechnology-introduction.htm> (December 1, 2006).

2. Quoted in Adam Keiper, "The Nanotechnology Revolution," *New Atlantis*, Summer 2003, reproduced in "Nanotechnology Press Kit: History of Nanotechnology," *Nanotechnology Now* Web site, <http://www.nanotech-now.com/Press_Kit/nanotechnology-history.htm> (December 1, 2006).

# Glossary

**acid**—A sour-tasting substance containing hydrogen; acids are one of the major classes of compounds in chemistry.

**atoms**—The basic building blocks of matter; each chemical element has a different kind of atom.

**calcining**—A process in which a metal combines with oxygen to produce a powdery substance.

**calorimeter**—A device that measures heat by measuring the amount of ice turned into liquid water.

**calx**—The product of calcining; a combination of a metal and oxygen.

**carbon dioxide**—A compound of carbon and oxygen ($CO_2$), usually seen as a gas; formerly called fixed air.

**chemical bond**—The force that holds atoms in a molecule together.

**combustion**—Burning; a process in which a nonmetal combines with oxygen.

**commune**—An independent city government.

**compound**—A substance containing two or more elements.

**convulsions**—Fits or seizures in which the body shakes uncontrollably.

**DNA**—A chemical in cells that carries coded instructions for making proteins and other processes.

**element**—A substance that cannot be broken down into other substances.

**Estates-General**—A lawmaking body in France, something like Congress in the United States or Parliament in Britain.

**Farmer-General**—In eighteenth-century France, a chief official of the Tax Farm.

**fixed air**—Old name for carbon dioxide.

**genus**—Group to which a living thing belongs; an example is *Canis*, the genus of dogs.

**geology**—The science that studies the earth.

**gross national product**—The value of the goods and services produced by a nation's people during a certain amount of time.

**guillotine**—An instrument of execution in which a large, slanted blade drops down to cut off someone's head.

**gypsum**—A mineral that is heated and then combined with water to make a plaster that hardens quickly.

**hydrogen**—An element, found alone usually as an inflammable gas; it also occurs in many compounds, including water, acids, and compounds from living things.

**mercury**—A metal element, appearing as a silvery liquid at room temperature.

**metric system**—A system of weights and measures invented in France in the late eighteenth century and widely used today.

**molecular manufacturing**—A form of nanotechnology that uses computer programs to make products by putting atoms and molecules together.

**molecule**—A combination of two or more atoms, held together by chemical bonds.

**nanobot**—A nanoscale-sized robot that can manufacture products by moving atoms and molecules.

**nanometer**—A billionth of a meter, or 0.00000004 inch.

**nanoparticle**—A particle between one and one hundred nanometers long.

**nanoscale technology**—Technology that makes products containing nanoparticles; it does not usually use the particles for manufacturing.

**nanotechnology**—A new field of science and technology that deals with very small particles and the possibility of using them for manufacturing.

**niter**—Potassium nitrate; used in making gunpowder.

**niter bed**—A ditch filled with manure and rotting plants, used to make saltpeter artificially.

**nitrogen**—An element, found alone as a colorless, odorless gas that makes up about four fifths of the atmosphere; it cannot support burning or breathing; it also exists in many compounds, including many found in living organisms.

**organic chemistry**—The study of compounds containing carbon and hydrogen, most of which come from living organisms.

**oxygen**—An element, found alone as a colorless, odorless gas that makes up about one fifth of the atmosphere; it combines with substances during burning, calcining, and respiration.

**proteins**—Complex chemicals that do most of the work in living bodies; cells make them by a natural form of molecular manufacturing.

**quantum effects**—Results of laws of physics that apply only to the particles inside atoms.

**Reign of Terror**—A period (1793–1794) during the French Revolution in which large numbers of people were executed with little or no trial and little or no evidence.

**respiration**—A chemical reaction in living organisms in which carbon-containing compounds from food combine with oxygen to produce heat, carbon dioxide, and water; also, breathing.

**Revolutionary Tribunal**—Special court that, during the French Revolution, tried people accused of crimes.

**RNA**—A chemical in cells that carries coded instructions for making proteins and other processes.

**saltpeter**—Substance formed naturally from minerals and manure or rotting plant matter; used as a source of niter for gunpowder.

**species**—A particular type of living organism.

**Tax Farm**—In eighteenth-century France, a private company to which the government leased, or farmed out, the right to collect certain taxes.

# Further Reading

## Books

Beckett, M. A., and A. W. G. Platt. *The Periodic Table at a Glance.* Cambridge, Mass.: Blackwell, 2006.

Cullen, Katherine. *Chemistry: The People Behind the Science.* New York: Facts on File, 2005.

Garrett, Ginger. *Solids, Liquids, and Gases.* New York: Scholastic/Children's Press, 2005.

Kjelle, Marylou Morano. *Antoine Lavoisier: Father of Chemistry.* Bear, Del.: Mitchell Lane, 2004.

Summers, Marilee. *C Is for Carbon.* West Chicago, Ill.: MackStorm Productions, 2006.

## Internet Addresses

**American Chemical Society**
http://acswebcontent.acs.org/kids/index.html

**Chem4Kids**
http://www.chem4kids.com

**Chemistry**
http://www.surfnetkids.com/chemistry.htm

# Index

**DATE DUE**

| | | | |
|---|---|---|---|
| | | | |
| | | | |
| | | | |
| | | | |
| | | | |
| | | | |
| | | | |
| | | | |
| | | | |

DEMCO 128-5046